# Religious Designs for Needlework

## Adalee Winter

Oxmoor House, Inc., Birmingham

Library of Congress Catalog Card Number: 77-74196

ISBN: 0-8487-0470-3

Manufactured in the United States of America

First Printing 1977


*Religious Designs for Needlework*

Editor: Mary Elizabeth Johnson
Photography: David Matthews
Copying of black and white charts: Andrew T. Brown

The author wishes to thank the following people
who made the projects for photography: Tappy
Folts, Fran Gregg, Jean Gordon, Mary Leta
Taylor, Meg Moeller, Gay Antrim, Connie Lee,
Terri Winter, Ann Curry, Ann Adair.

# Contents

There are many places in a church where needlework can be used either to enhance the beauty of the interior or to add to the meaning of the service. From left:

The grapes and vine from pages 6 through 9 are worked on a cloth for the communion service in cross stitch on Aida cloth. A bookmark is worked in needlepoint with embroidery floss and has a small cross in a circle from page 37. A minister's stole is cross stitched on Aida cloth in the fleur-de-lis design from page 16. A needlepoint kneeler worked in tapestry yarn utilizes three different designs, found on pages 12, 13, and 15, plus the border from pages 14–15. Inside the offering plate is a small pad worked in needlepoint with embroidery floss, featuring the fish design from page 19.

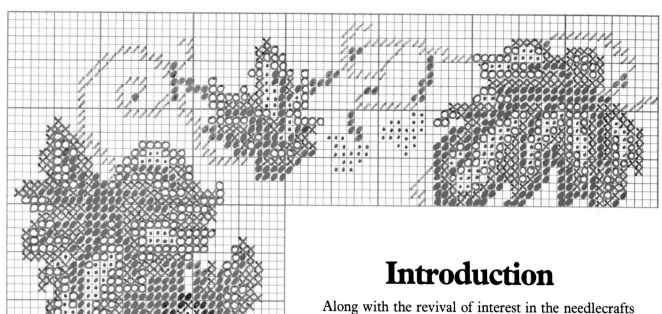

# Introduction

Along with the revival of interest in the needlecrafts of our grandmothers, there is a renewal of interest in the values they held dear. For example, an open expression of religious faith is admired now, as it was then. This may be part of the joy of living in our time—we will experience a return to simple expressions of values; we will know the joy of creating with our own hands; and we will have the luxury of doing old crafts more easily with new techniques and materials.

This book is presented with the hope that you will use it to stitch projects that you can use either in your home or in your place of worship. The lore of religious symbolism is so rich and diverse that it invites many different interpretations; thus, there are many different styles represented here, in a range to suit traditionalists as well as those with more contemporary tastes. There are designs from both the Old and the New Testaments, but many of the designs are not obviously and exclusively religious emblems—the grapes, wheat, flowers, animals, borders, and alphabets, for example. Needlecraft enthusiasts who are not interested in the religious meanings can still enjoy the color, complexity, and majesty of these designs.

The charts included in this book can be used with your favorite needlecraft technique—be it needlepoint, cross stitch, knitting, piecing and quilting, even bead-

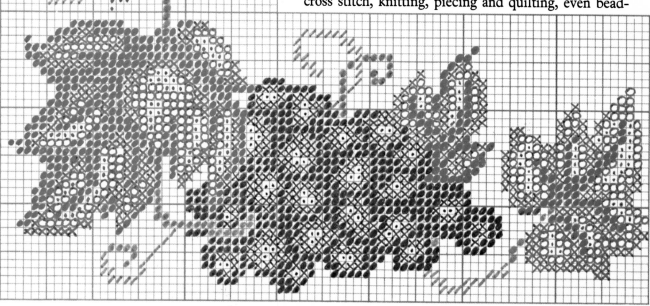

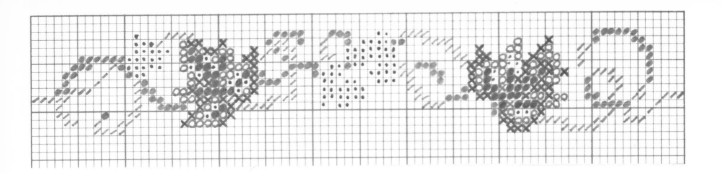

work. Many of the projects we have photographed are done in needlepoint or counted-thread embroidery, but you may want to try your hand at other projects, such as knitting a scarf which incorporates some of the little symbols on pages 36-37. Or, you can make beautiful Chrismon ornaments by gluing beads to graph paper, then cutting the paper away close to the outside beads. The choice of material and technique is up to you.

When considering which projects you want to make with these beautiful designs, look around your home and consider how your life might be enriched by living every day with some reminder of your religious faith. Some of the possibilities for projects are table linens, wall hangings, pillows, book covers, bookmarks, and clothing. The vivid colors and intricate design of these religious emblems, when used in home decoration, can stimulate religious discussions, even with very young children. See the suggestions at the end of this section for planning needlework projects.

If you are one of a congregation of a church who wishes to give of your time and talent to make a lasting contribution, you might consider forming a group to work such projects as kneeling cushions, altar rails, chair seats, book covers, bookmarks, lectern hangings, banners, and communion linens. Here are some suggestions to make group work easier.

1. Consider retaining a qualified needleworker to teach basic stitches to those interested in working on the project. Some in your congregation may not have done needlework but would like to participate. You will, of course, want to maintain a consistently high standard

of quality, no matter how many people work on the project. Much needlework, especially needlepoint, will endure for many generations, and if it's not of the highest quality, you will begin to wish it weren't so durable!

2. It is also a good idea to have all the persons who wish to work on the project submit samples of their work, such as a one-inch square worked in tent stitch. Everyone interested in the project should work this one-inch square. The squares can then be numbered, and someone outside the congregation can select the samples which are of high quality and look like one another. The finished project should look as though one person worked it. The selection of needleworkers should be kept as impersonal as possible to insure the best needlework with the least friction within your congregation.

3. You will inevitably have some workers who say they cannot work from a chart. They will want a painted canvas. Try a little gentle persuasion, explaining that to follow a chart, you make one stitch over each intersection on the canvas. Explain that even properly painted canvases, done with permanent ink markers or acrylics, will bleed colors into the yarn if improperly blocked. This is because the sizing in the canvas is water soluble. If the permanently colored sizing floats loose from the canvas and gets into the yarn, neither washing, dry cleaning, spot removing, or prayer will remove the color from the yarn. Another advantage of working from a chart is that the intersections of the canvas are easier to see when they are not the same

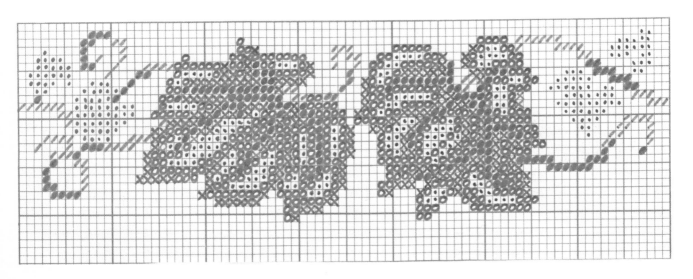

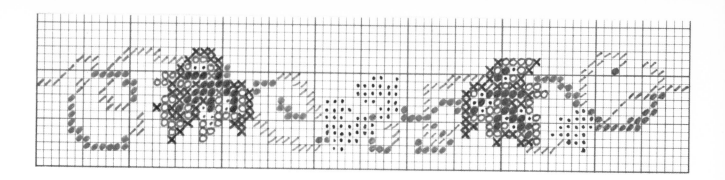

color as the yarn. This insures that stitches will not be skipped.

**4.** If you are in charge of planning the projects your group will work for the church or temple, you will be responsible for selecting the style, colors, and theme of the designs. Your place of worship already has a style of decor, ranging from naive to baroque or gothic to ultra-modern. Your needlework should blend well with this style. There are a variety of styles within this book, but you may wish to make particular designs more elaborate or more stylized to suit your particular theme. Find someone in your church membership who has artistic talent and will enjoy working with you to adapt these designs to your particular needs.

You may decide to have your needlework designs revolve around a central theme. Your church name may suggest what the theme should be. A church of the Holy Cross might use the various styles of crosses; Christ Church may use the symbols which represent Christ; or a Trinity Church could use symbols of God, the Holy Spirit, Christ, and the Trinity.

Color is very important in every needlework project you plan. The background color of the needlework should blend well with the colors of the walls, the carpet, and other furnishings. (Consider also the church windows if they are of colored glass.) The liturgical colors are white, red, green, violet, and black. In most cases, these colors, plus gold, which represents the majesty of God, are used in the designs, especially if the needlework is planned specifically for a church. You may, of course, use the lights and darks of each of these colors, as well as either a bright, vivid color range or a subdued, muted palette. Each needlework piece should have one very light and one very dark color, with the other colors ranging from very light to very dark.

You must also decide whether or not you want borders on your design. Borders may enclose the central design on top of a kneeling cushion or on a banner, or a border may be worked around the sides of a boxed kneeler. You will notice that many border designs are included in the book. These borders are not intended specifically or exclusively for the designs with which they are shown; rather, you should treat them as complete designs of their own, to be used where you choose.

As to the technical considerations of planning a project, you will find that you have to count on doing a lot of measuring of areas and counting of threads to determine the size of finished pieces. In addition, you should, *when planning the project,* talk to a finisher—the person who can block your needlework and sew it into a finished piece. This person can tell you such things as how much seam allowance to leave, advise you as to how to block kneelers, hang wall banners, and tell you other important details you must consider before you start stitching. It is a good rule of thumb that the fewer seams used, the greater the strength and durability of the finished work.

We wish you great joy in expressing your faith with your needlework, and hope for you that the finished work will be beautiful, last forever, and be a source of happiness to all who see it.

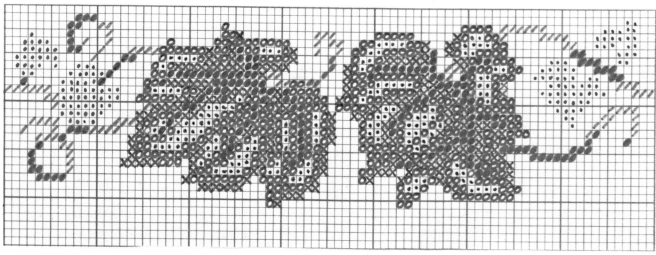

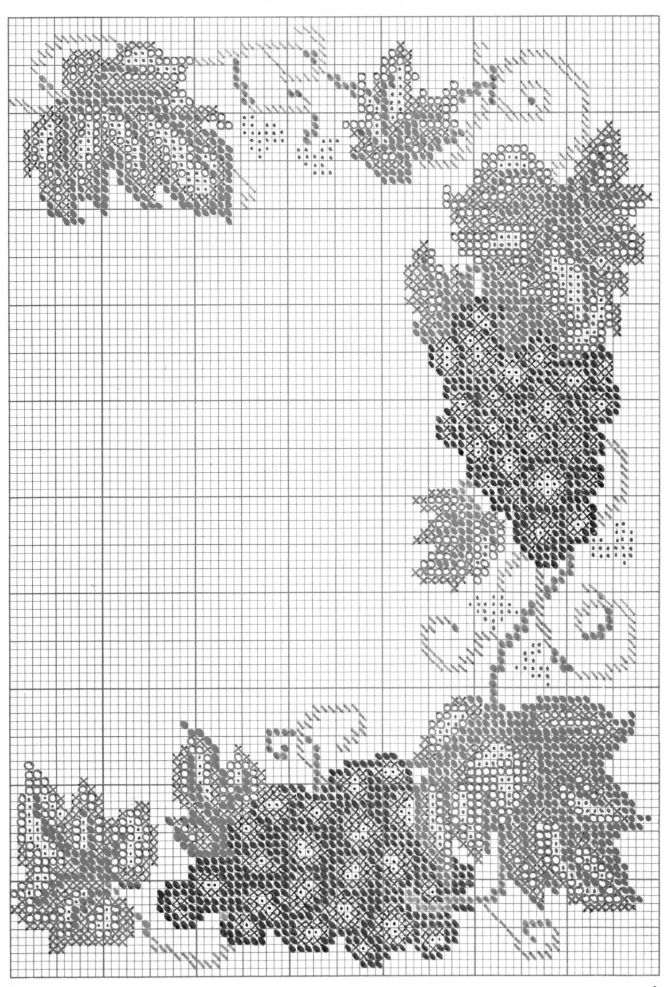

# Meaning of Symbols and Emblems

Religious symbols and emblems offer, in addition to their outstanding beauty, a comforting reminder of our individual faith because of the concepts they represent. The strictest interpretations of the meanings of the various symbols and emblems may be learned through private research and through studies in the teaching programs of your church or synagogue; we offer here the broadest, most generally applicable meanings of the different symbols and emblems included in this book. It is interesting to note that many of the symbols came about as a result of the need for secrecy among the early practitioners of specific religions. Also, many of the symbols of the Christian and Jewish faiths are the same when they represent something from the Old Testament.

*Grapes and Vine:* (pages 6-9, and 37): In the Old Testament, the grapes and vine stand for entry into the Promised Land. In the New Testament, they are the symbol for the blood of Christ, the Last Supper, Holy Communion.

*Chi Rho* (pages 12 and 36): The Greek letter *chi* looks like the English letter X; The Greek letter *rho* looks like the English letter P. These are the first two letters in the Greek spelling of Christ.

*Crown and Cross* (pages 13 and 37): The crown denotes the majesty of God; the cross represents Christ and faith in Him.

*Cross and Descending Dove* (pages 14 and 37): The cross is the central theme of the Christian faith because the crucifixion of Christ led to the resurrection which is the basis for the Christian belief in eternal life. The descending dove always stands for the Holy Spirit, as at Christ's baptism or at Pentecost.

*IHS* (pages 15, 36, and 46): The first letters of Jesus Hominum Salvator, Jesus Saviour of Men, in Greek.

*Fleur-de-Lis* (page 16): A stylized iris flower whose three petals represent the Trinity—Father, Son, and Holy Spirit.

*Five-pointed Star* (page 17): In Old Testament terminology, the star stands for Man. In the New Testament, it stands for the Star of Bethlehem or of the Magi, which led the three kings to Christ's birthplace.

*Chalice* (pages 17 and 37): The cup from which Christ drank at the Last Supper; the Holy Grail of medieval legend; Holy Communion.

*Agnus Dei* (page 18): The Lamb of God with the banner of victory. It represents Christ victorious over sin and death, a New Testament belief that Christ was without sin and lives forever.

*Triquetra and Circle* (page 19): Three denotes the Trinity—Father, Son, and Holy Spirit: the circle stands for eternity, as it is without beginning or end.

*Three Fish in a Circle* (page 19): Again the circle means eternity. The fish is one of the earliest symbols of Christ, based on an acrostic spelling of Christ. (See page 36 also). Three represents the Trinity: Father, Son and Holy Spirit.

*Escallop Shell with Drops of Water* (page 19): Christ's baptism.

*Book* (pages 20 and 37): The Scriptures, or God speaking to man through the written word.

*Lamp* (pages 20 and 37): Truth, understanding, faith.

*Crown of Thorns* (page 21): Martyrdom, the majesty of Christ as God's Son; His suffering.

*Ship on a Stormy Sea with Descending Dove* (pages 21 and 36): The ship represents the congregation of believers; the stormy sea represents troubled times; the descending dove is the help of the Holy Spirit.

*The Sheaf of Wheat* (page 22): In the Old Testament, the giving of the Law at Sinai; the Feast of the Pentecost. The New Testament meaning is the Last Supper.

*Scroll* (pages 11 and 23): An earlier form of codex, or book; the five books of Moses; the first five books of the Old Testament; the Torah, the most sacred law of the Jews.

*Tablets of Stone* (page 23): The Ten Commandments; the laws given to Moses by God on Mount Sinai.

*Dove with Olive Branch* (page 24): Peace, forgiveness, hope, purity.

*Noah's Ark* (page 24): The flood, and God's help to those who believe in Him; a refuge from peril; faith. The rainbow symbolizes God's love and protection.

*Flaming Sword* (page 25): Expulsion; a broken relationship with God. The sword guarded the path to the Tree of Life after Adam and Eve were expelled from the Garden of Eden.

*Seven-branched Candelabra* (page 25): Known as the Menorah, it is a symbol of Jewish faith. It symbolizes the presence of God in the temple, home, or church.

*Triangle* (page 36): Another symbol for the Trinity: Father, Son and Holy Spirit.

*Alpha and Omega* (page 37): The Greek letter *alpha* is an A; it represents the beginning; the Greek letter *omega* looks like an upside-down U and symbolizes the end. The letters stand for God as the beginning and the end of all things.

*The Lion* (pages 44–45); Majesty, power, strength.

*The Lamb* (page 60): Purity, innocence, gentleness.

## Religious Symbolism of Colors and Flowers

The liturgical colors and the concepts they are each generally regarded to represent:

*Red:* The Old Testament meaning is of life; the New Testament meaning is of martyrdom.

*Blue:* Heavenly love.

*White:* Holiness and purity; innocence.

*Green:* Regeneration; renewal.

*Violet:* Royalty.

*Gold:* Majesty of God.

*Black:* Sleep and rest.

The popular symbolism of the selected flowers illustrated in this book is as follows:

*Acanthus Leaves* (page 31): Usually shown very stylized, they represent heaven.

*Pomegranate* (page 54, top): The resurrection: immortality.

*Lotus* (page 54, bottom): The hope that the faithful have of triumph over adversity.

*Rose* (page 55, top): The Nativity; Messianic prophecy; love.

*Lily* (page 55, bottom): Humility, purity; immortality. The lily is often used as the symbol of the Virgin.

*Violet* (page 56, top): The humility of the Son of God.

*Daisy* (page 56, bottom): The innocence of the Holy Child.

*Columbine* (page 57, top): The seven gifts of the Holy Spirit— see Revelation 5:12.

*Passion Flower* (page 57, bottom): Christ's disciples and His crucifixion.

Color code on page 16

Color code on page 16

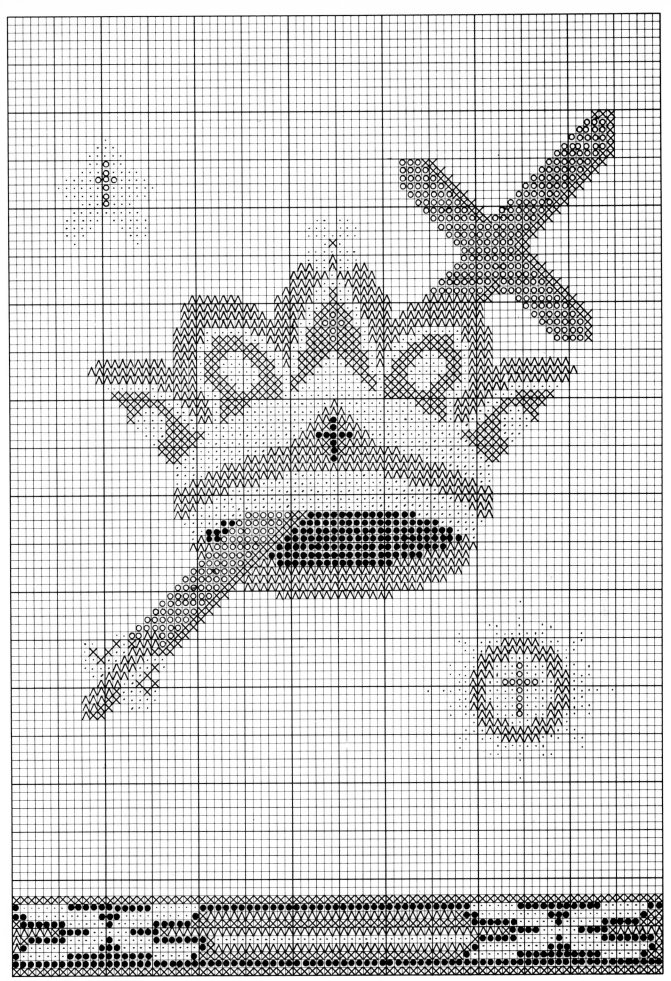

Color code on page 16

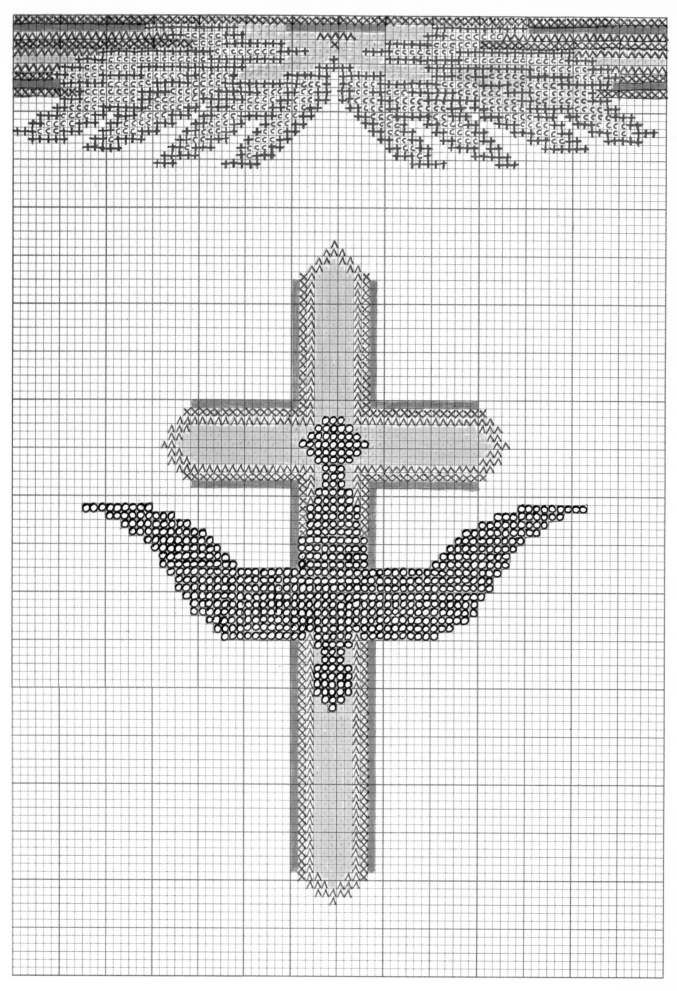

14

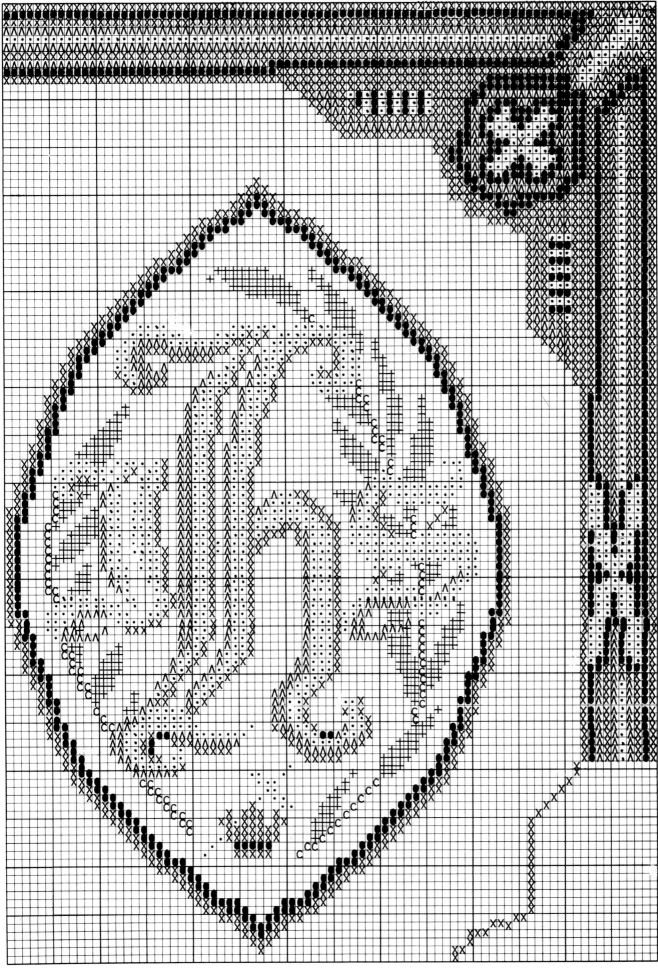

Color code on page 16

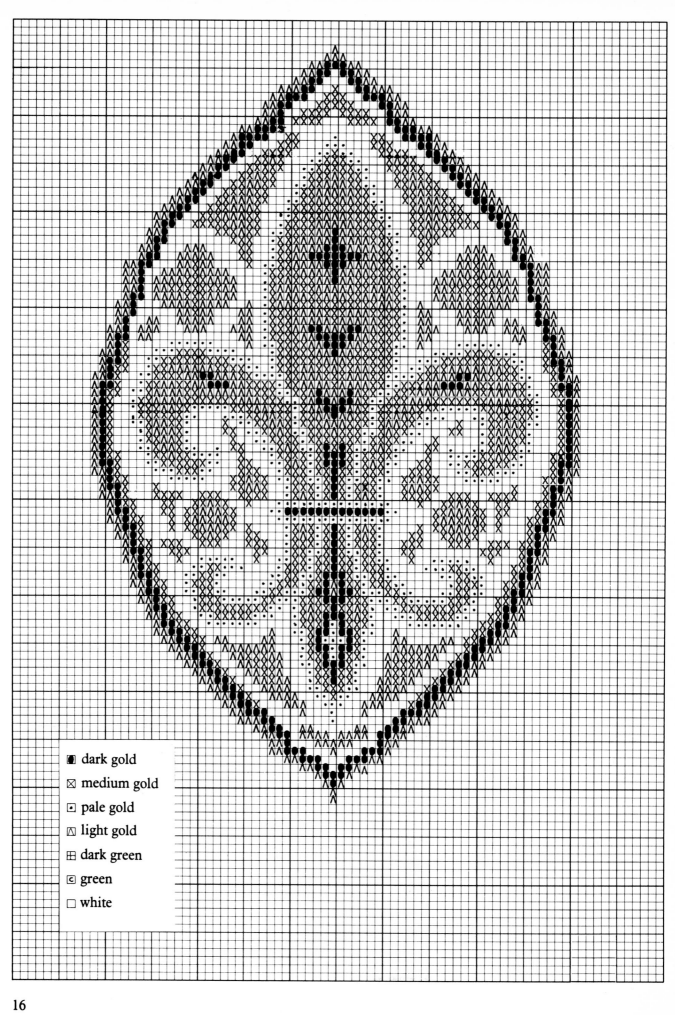

● dark gold
⊠ medium gold
⊡ pale gold
⋀ light gold
⊞ dark green
ⓒ green
□ white

16

18

Color code on page 16

Color code on page 16

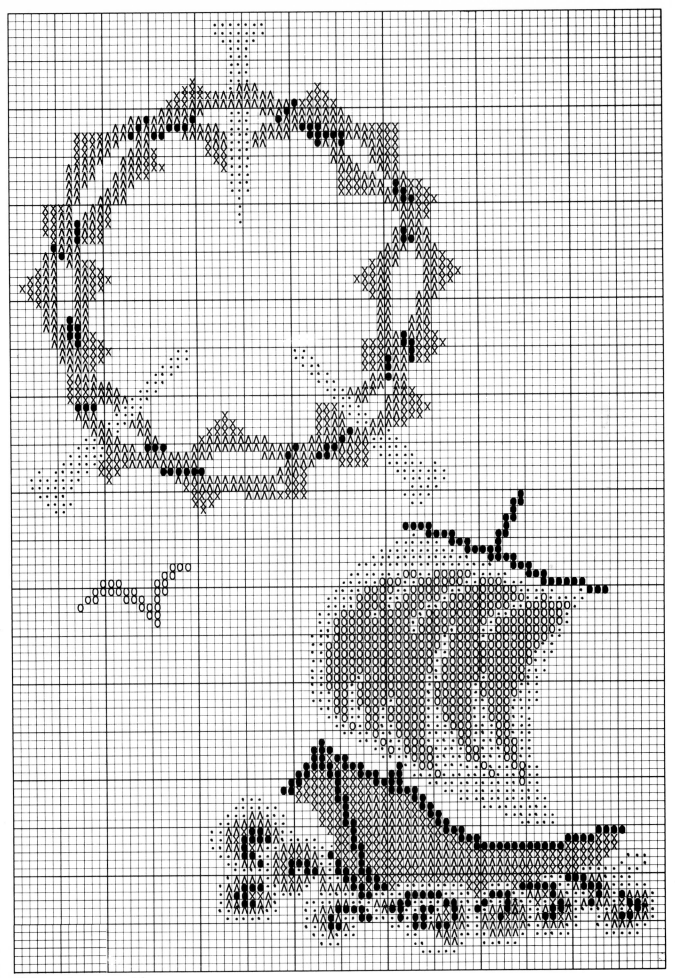

Color code on page 16

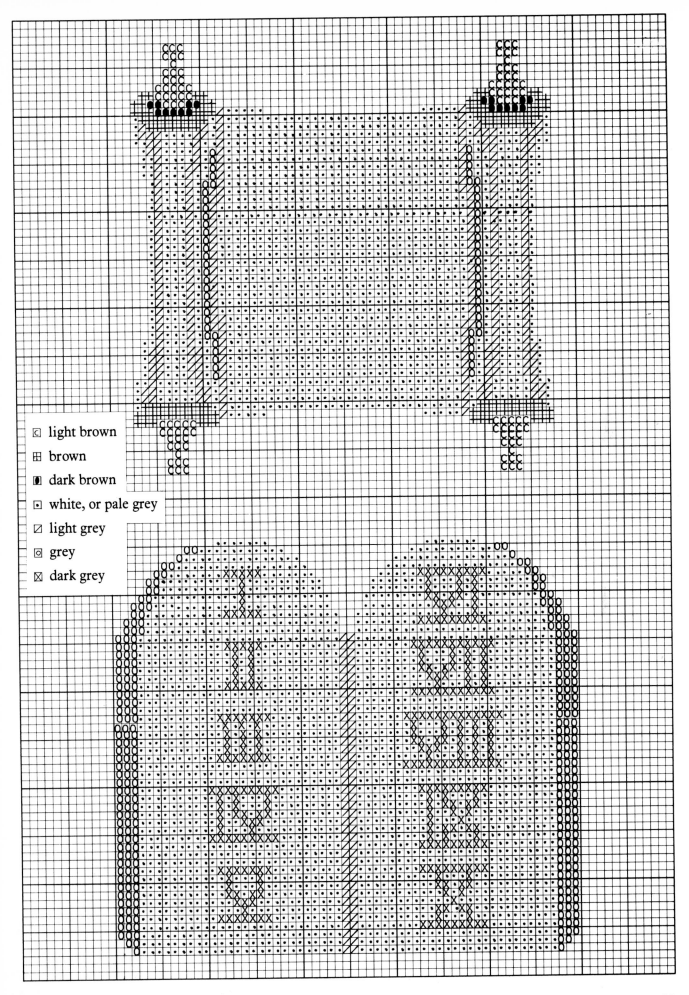

□ light brown
⊞ brown
◑ dark brown
⊡ white, or pale grey
⊿ light grey
◉ grey
⊠ dark grey

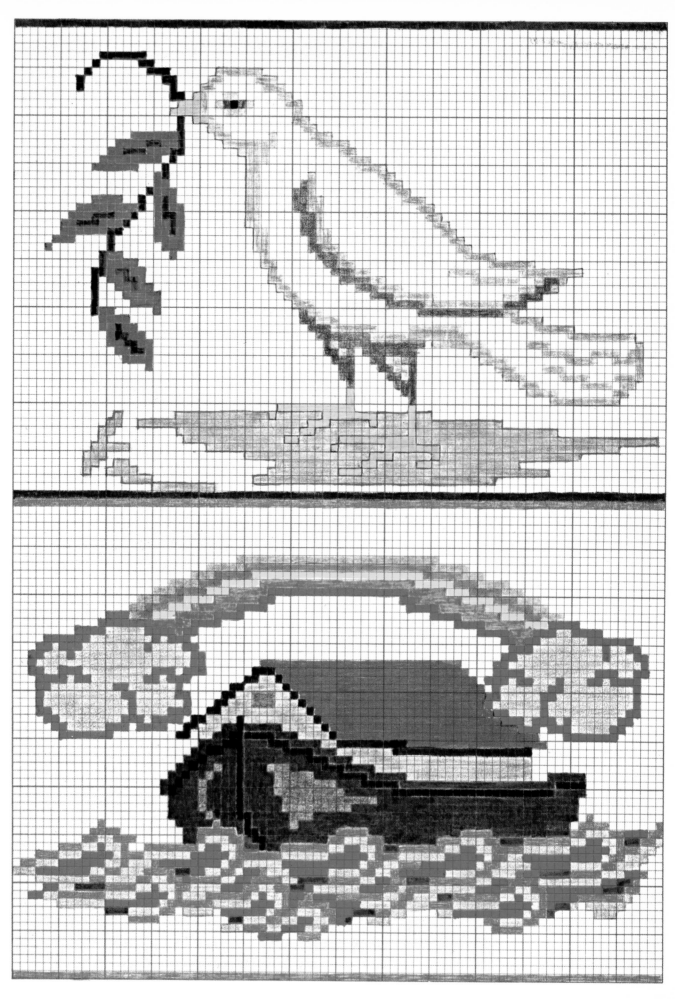

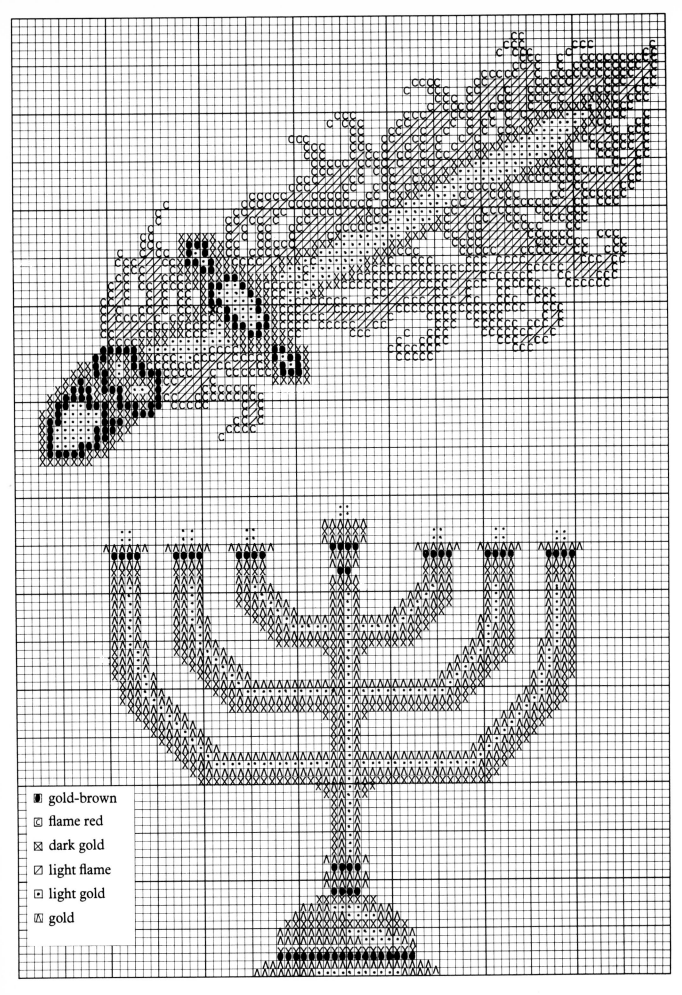

- ◖ gold-brown
- Ⓒ flame red
- ⊠ dark gold
- ◪ light flame
- ⊡ light gold
- ⋀ gold

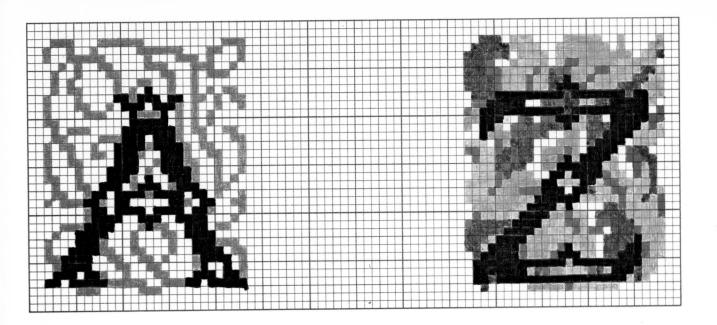

Before the invention of the printing press, books had to be copied by hand. This was a long and laborious process, and it gave rise to a guild of specialists in lettering. These specialists refined their skills to such a point that they created the beautifully intricate illuminated letters which are often associated with Bibles. The lettering of the older manuscripts became as much of an art form as was the actual text that was copied. Illuminated letters invoke almost automatically a religious connotation, even today.

The first alphabet which follows can be used one of two ways. The letters may be stitched alone, or you may stitch them over one of the illuminated backgrounds shown on pages 28, 29, 30, and 31, as illustrated here with the letters A and Z. Stitch the background completely first, then embroider the desired letter over it. Notice that each letter contains at least one little cross.

One suggestion for how these alphabets may be used is to choose a favorite Bible verse and stitch the first letter with the illuminated capital, then the remainder with the lowercase letters given on page 32. A less elaborate alphabet is given on page 31.

The Hebrew consonants are given on page 34 and the vowel sounds as worked with the consonant *daleth* are on page 35.

(*Note:* The illuminated letters I, H, and S for the first alphabet are given on page 46.)

---

*Table linens and accessories such as these serve as a gentle reminder of your faith to family and guests. A gerda cloth table runner, hem stitched all around, features a design from page 19, worked in cross stitch. Napkins in the same fabric could be monogrammed with your family initial, using one of the illuminated letters beginning on this page. The napkin rings are needlepoint, worked with tapestry yarn and highlighted with metallic yarn; each one features a different style of cross from page 38. The wheat design on page 22 seems particularly suited to a linen napkin for the bread basket, and is cross stitched.*

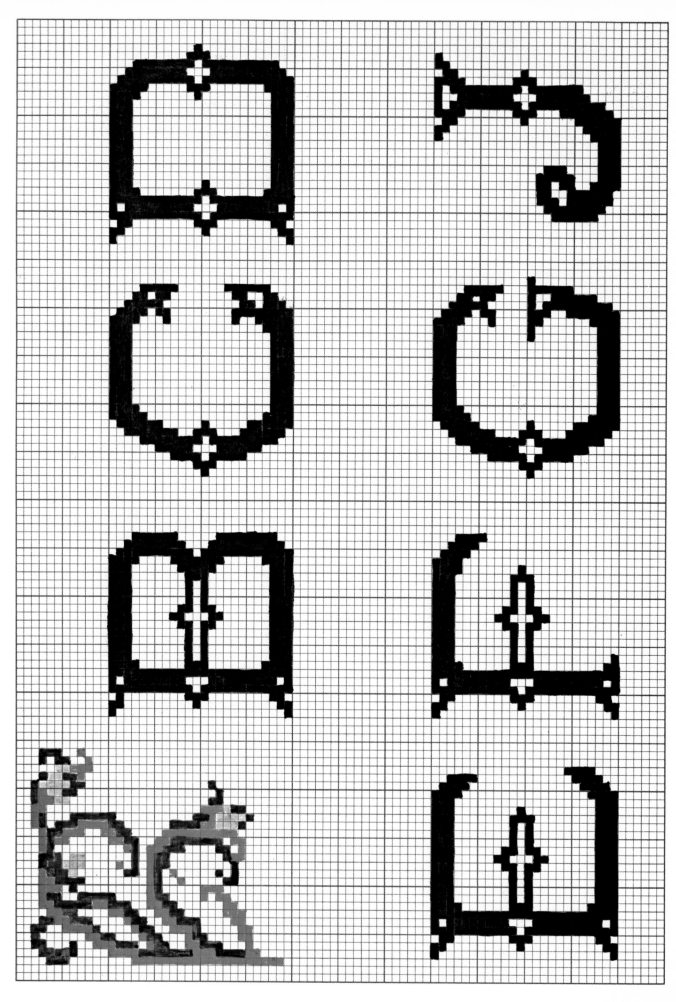

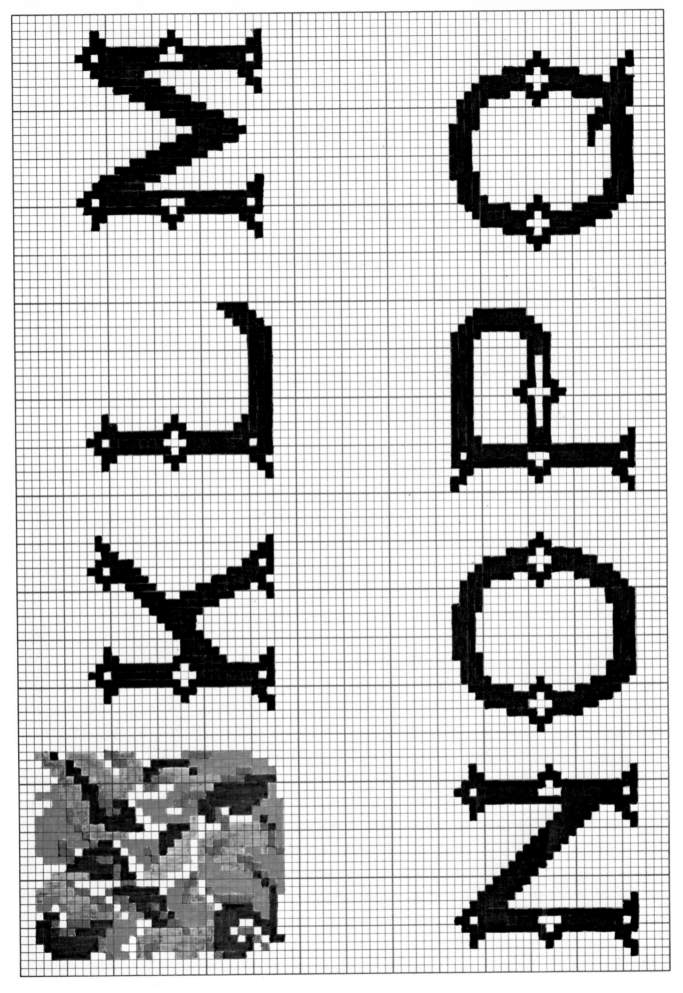

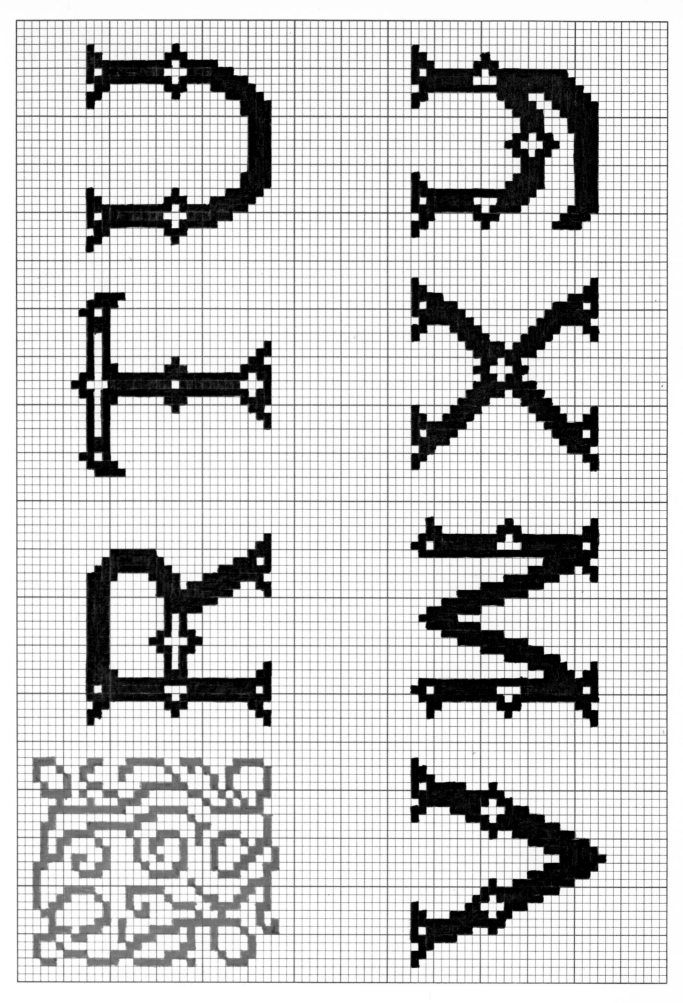

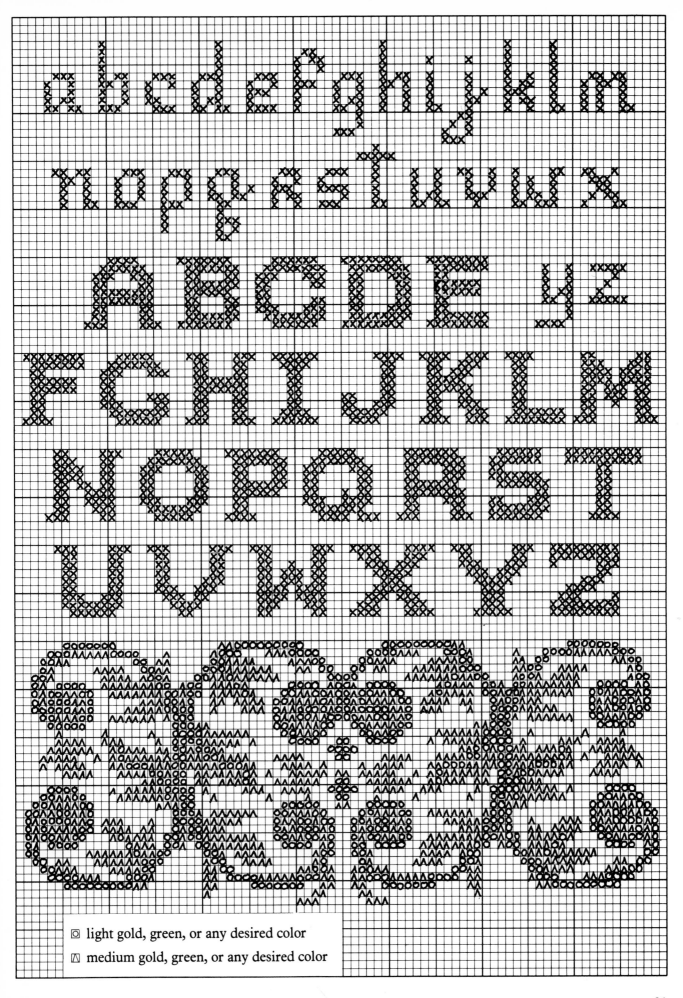

abcdefghijklm
nopqrstuvwx
yz

ABCDE
FGHIJKLM
NOPQRST
UVWXYZ

◎ light gold, green, or any desired color

⬚ medium gold, green, or any desired color

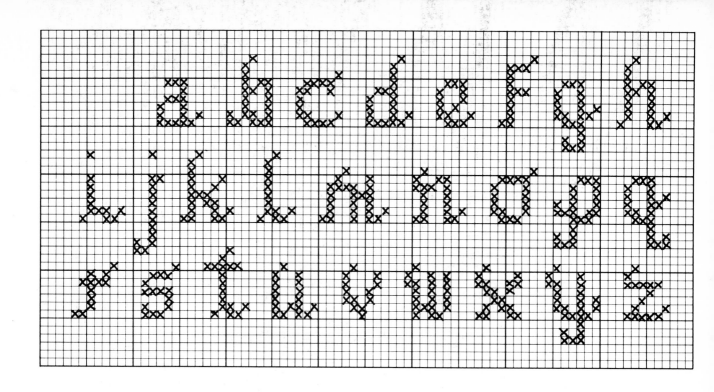

A pair of pillows with Noah's Ark and all the animals will surely delight any child! Please don't overlook the smallest animals—the dots in the lower left near the lion's foot are fleas! The animals from page 43 are stitched in needlepoint with tapestry yarn and the ark and rainbow from page 24 are worked on Aida cloth with embroidery floss. A rectangular pillow which could be used as a kneeling cushion for bedtime prayers features the lamb design from page 60 and is needlepointed with tapestry yarn. The bookmark is beadwork and uses the ship from page 21. A favorite child's prayer from pages 40–41 and the cherub from page 42 are worked on Aida cloth in cross stitch, then framed to hang on the wall.

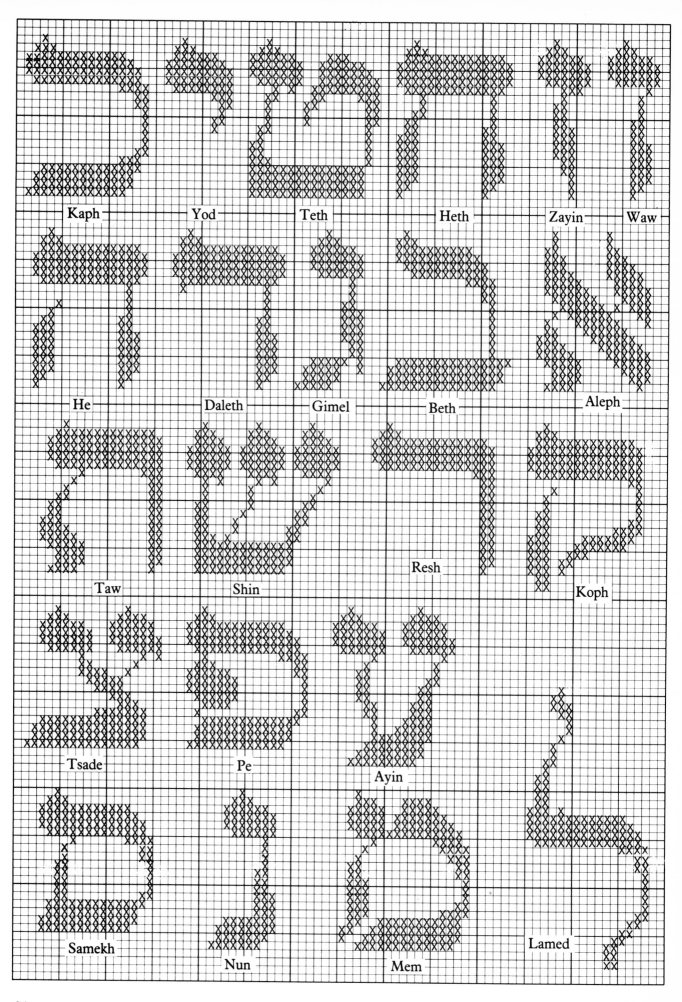

Kaph  Yod  Teth  Heth  Zayin  Waw

He  Daleth  Gimel  Beth  Aleph

Taw  Shin  Resh  Koph

Tsade  Pe  Ayin

Samekh  Nun  Mem  Lamed

34

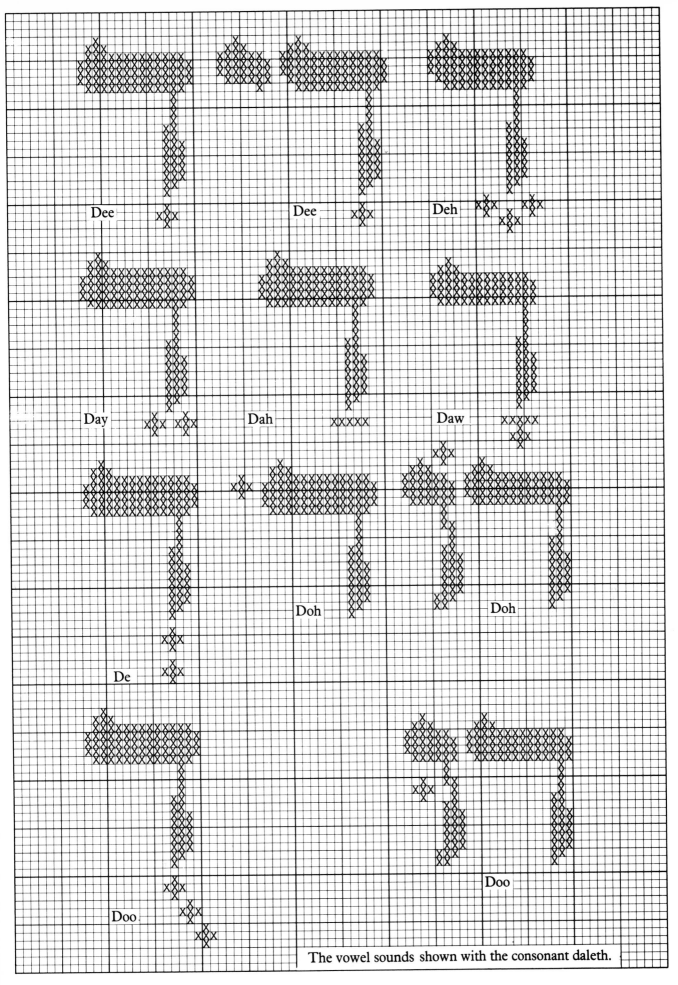

Dee

Dee

Deh

Day

Dah

Daw

De

Doh

Doh

Doo

Doo

The vowel sounds shown with the consonant daleth.

Color code on page 38 — for pages 36, 37

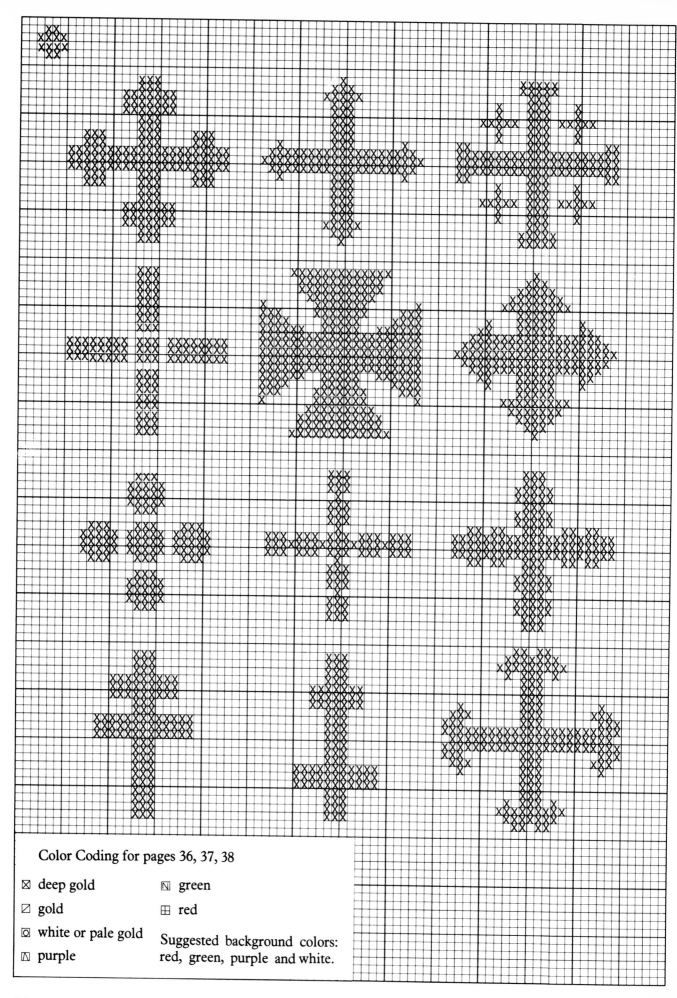

Color Coding for pages 36, 37, 38

⊠ deep gold          ◣ green

◪ gold               ⊞ red

◙ white or pale gold

◣ purple

Suggested background colors:
red, green, purple and white.

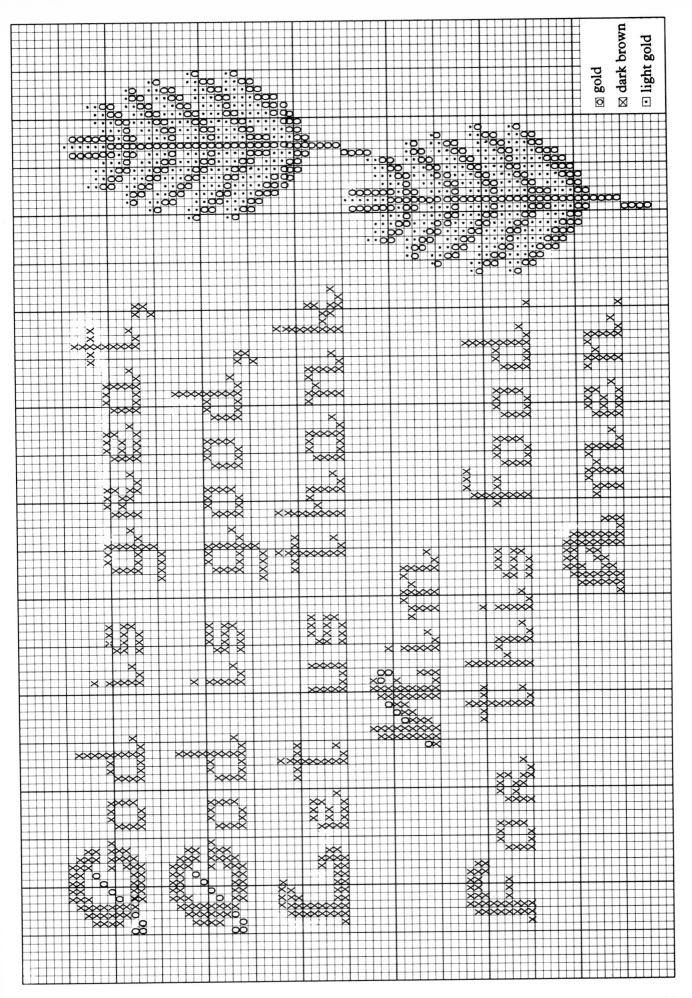

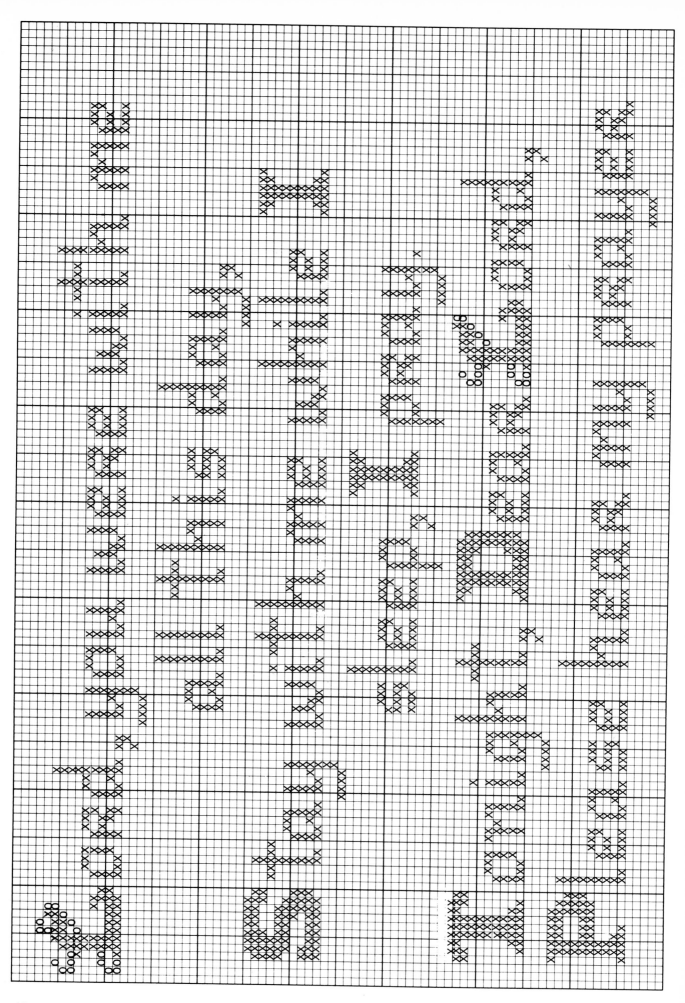

40

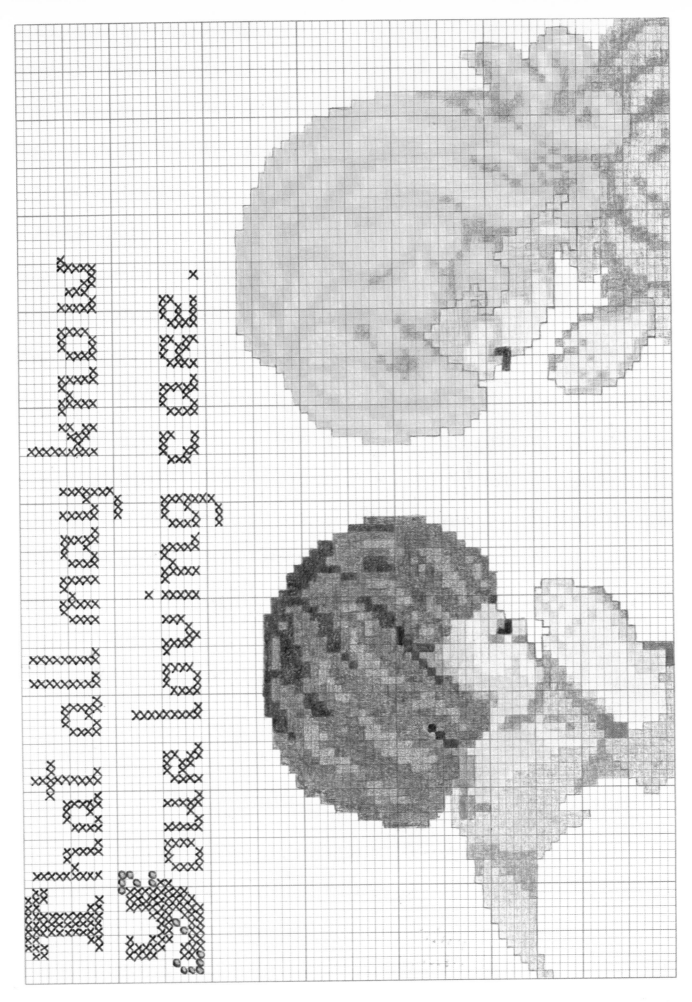

That all maximum

your normal care

41

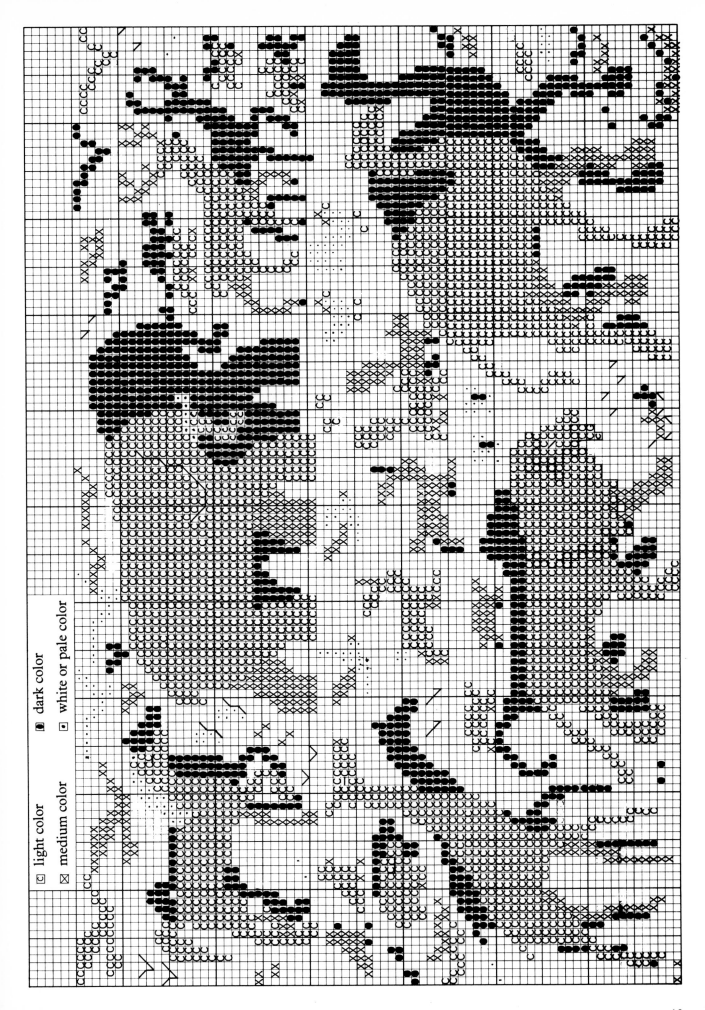

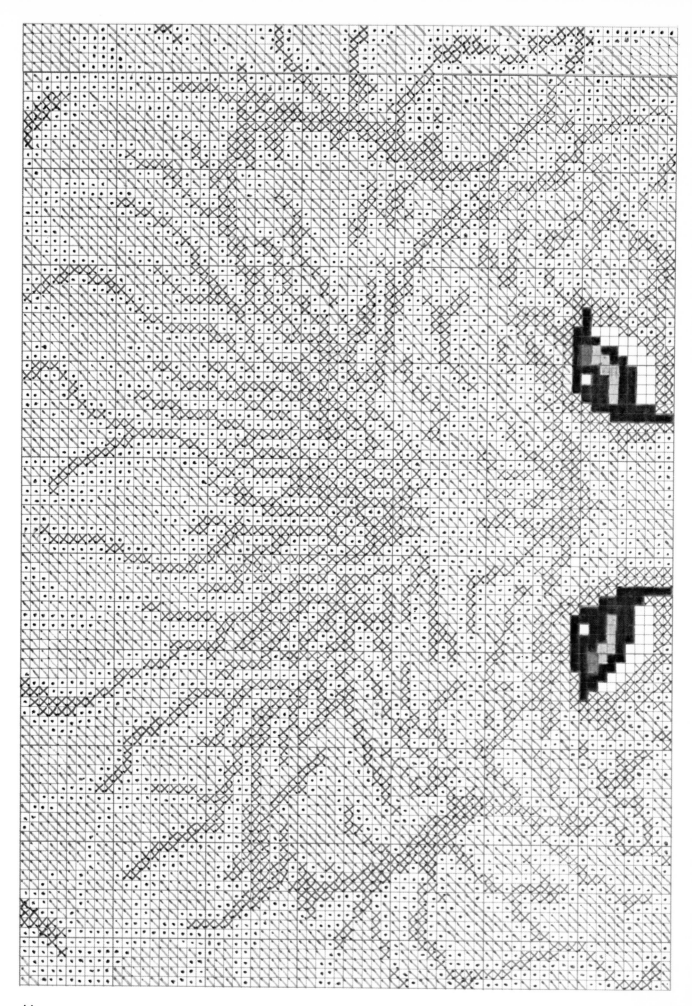

44

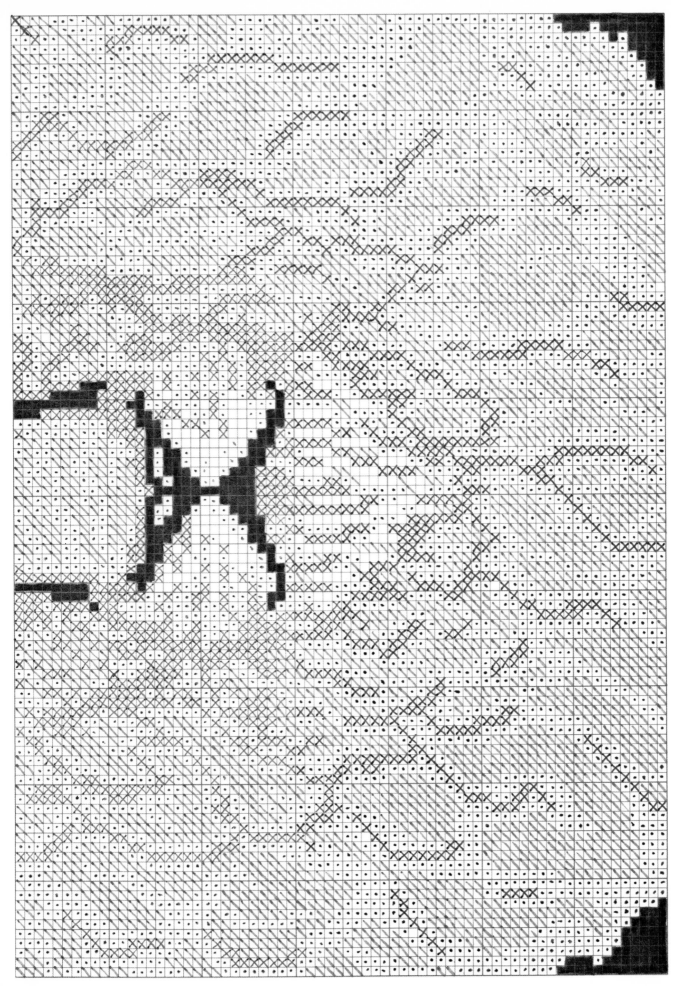

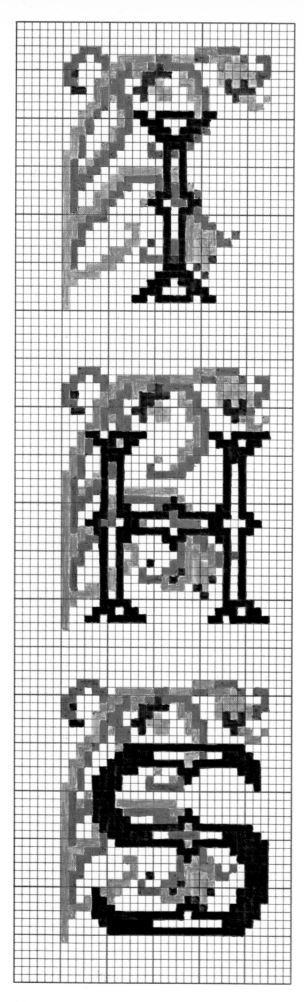

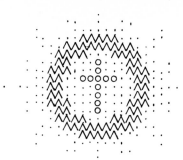

The cross has been used in almost every religion of the world in some form or another. In its earliest interpretation, the vertical line of the cross represented light from heaven, and the horizontal bar represented water. The crossing of the lines represented creation.

Although there are many different styles of crosses, the Latin cross is the one seen most often today. Most Protestants use an empty cross in their services to show that although Christ died, he rose to live forever. However, some Christians show a cross with a human form on it to recall Christ's suffering; this is called a crucifix.

During the time of the Crusades, several types of crosses became well recognized as symbolic of the mission of the crusaders. A cross which shows four smaller crosses at the intersection of the vertical and horizontal bars is known as the Jerusalem cross; four small crosses represent the four corners of the world. The cross Fitchy, which has four pointed ends, was also a crusader's cross, as it could be stuck in the ground anywhere it was needed. The Maltese cross looks like four spearheads of equal size which are placed with the points touching. The eight outer corners of a Maltese cross represent the Beatitudes.

Some crosses feature a circle, which goes through the vertical and horizontal bars. While the circle adds certain strength to the construction of the cross, the main purpose is the representation of eternal life. Known as the Celtic cross, it is often seen in cemeteries in Ireland as a reminder that the dead are with God.

In the Middle Ages especially, churches were built in the shape of a cross. This design is known as a cruciform, and it is the basis for most of the great cathedrals and is still used today in modified form for modern churches.

*An array of gifts and articles for special occasions gives an idea of the many ways these religious designs can be used. Counter-clockwise, from lower right:*

*A set of Chrismon ornaments, some of which are needlepointed with tapestry yarn while others are cross stitched on velvet, use the small symbols and emblems on pages 36-37. A Bible cover, needlepointed with tapestry yarn, makes beautiful use of the lily and rose designs on page 55. A small cross-stitched picture uses the angels on page 48 and is worked on Aida cloth. A ringbearer's pillow, also needlepointed with tapestry yarn, is worked in the columbine design from page 57. A cross from page 38 to be worn as a pendant is done in beadwork. One of a set of coasters in the acanthus leaf design from page 31 is needlepoint worked in tapestry yarn.*

⊡ pale yellow, blue, gold or other background color    ⊠ blue

⊚ flesh                               ☐ white

⊠ black                           backstitching—black

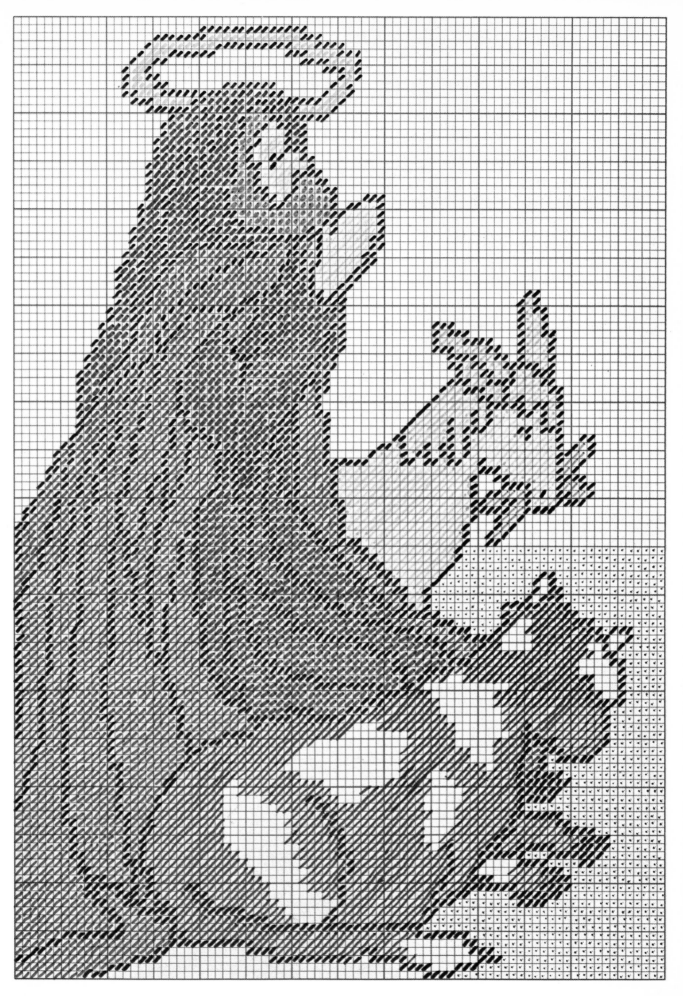

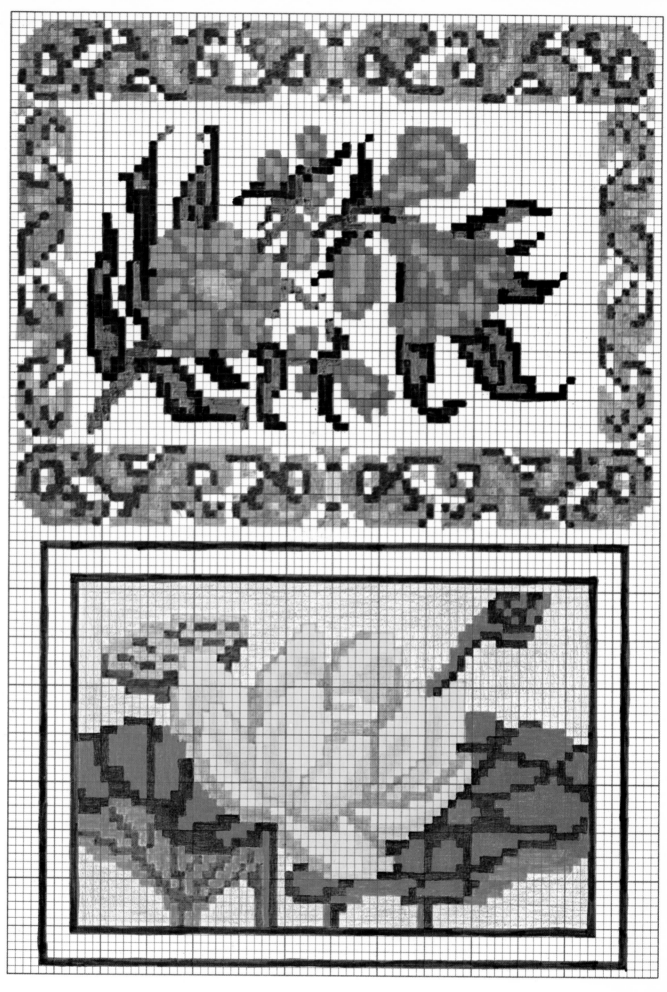

54

58

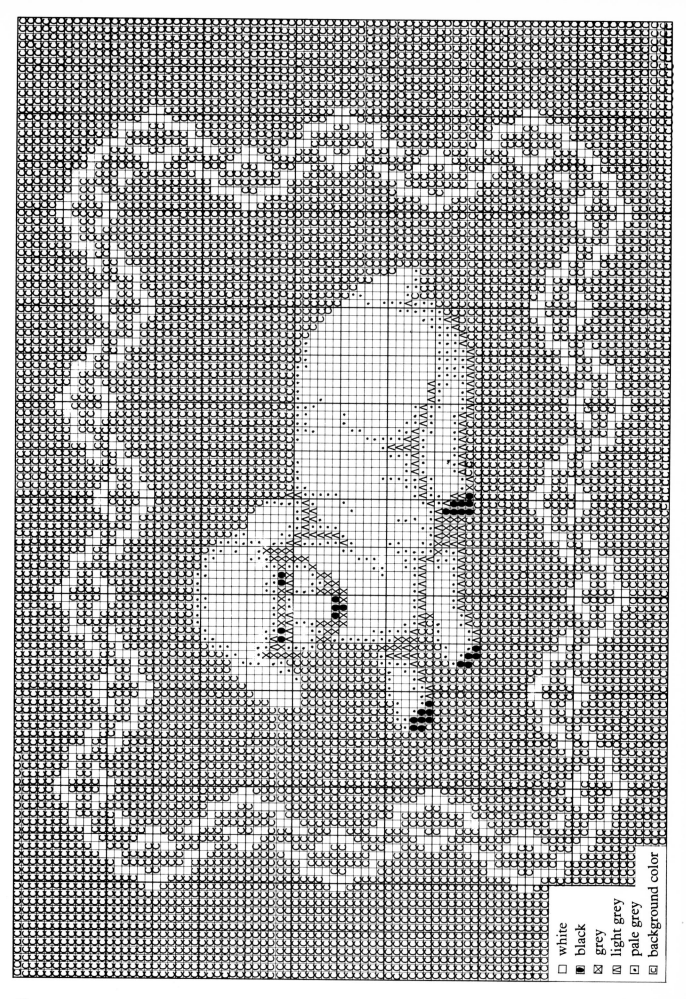

| | white |
|---|---|
| ■ | black |
| ⊠ | grey |
| ☒ | light grey |
| ⊡ | pale grey |
| ☉ | background color |

60

# How To Work from a Charted Design

Please note that the words *graph* and *chart* are used interchangeably. They mean the same thing. The most important thing to remember in working with a charted design is that *each square on the graph represents one stitch.*

*To determine the size of a finished piece* that will be worked by following a graph, count the squares in the height and width of the design. Some of the charts in this book have twelve squares in an inch, with a darker line every sixth intersection, and some have ten squares to the inch, with every fifth intersection line darker. No matter how many squares there are in an inch on the graph, the design can be stitched on a canvas or fabric of any mesh you choose. (Mesh is the number of stitches allowed for in an inch of fabric or canvas.) A design charted on twelve squares to the inch graph paper may be stitched on ten mesh needlepoint canvas, 22 mesh quickpoint canvas, 14 mesh Aida cloth, 5 mesh quick point canvas, or any other mesh canvas or cloth that you want to use. The fact that the chart shows twelve squares in an inch does not affect the size of the finished work . . . the number of stitches that you work in an inch determines the finished size.

Mathematics can be irritating when you are anxious to begin stitching, but it is necessary. If you do not figure carefully at the outset, you may find that you have bought much more material than you needed, or, much worse, that your stitches run off the edge of the material. In this case, the whole piece will have to be discarded and begun again. Here is a useful formula:

The number of squares in the height of the graphed design

divided by

the number of stitches in an inch of your needlework

equals

the number of inches high the stitched design will be.

The same formula works for determining the width.

When you know how long and how wide your stitched design will be, you must then allow extra material around the edges for whatever you wish for background, plus 1 to 1½ inches all around for finishing.

*Example:* A charted design counts 120 squares high by 84 squares wide. To work in needlepoint on 12 mesh canvas, divide 120 by 12 and 84 by 12. The design will work out to be 10 inches high and 7 inches wide. If you want 1 additional inch of background stitches all around, the finished piece will measure 9 by 12 inches. Add 1½ inches for finishing; you will need a piece of canvas that measures 12 by 15 inches.

To work the same design in cross stitch on 22 mesh hardanger cloth, divide 120 by 22 and 84 by 22. Your answer will be 5.45 inches high and 3.8 inches wide. Round off the figures to 5½ by 4 inches. If you want an additional ½ inch all around for background material, the finished piece will measure approximately 6½ by 5 inches. Add 1½ inches all around for finishing and you know you will need a piece of hardanger cloth that measures 9½ by 8 inches.

*To begin stitching from a charted design,* remember that one square on the graph paper represents one stitch. If you have never worked from a chart, your first look at so many small squares of different colors or color symbols may discourage you. But, if you can see to do needlework, you can see well enough to follow a chart. The grids of the chart are not smaller than the mesh of the canvas or cloth you work on.

There are, however, ways to make counting the squares in the chart easier. A stitch finder is used with the chart; it has metal strips that you line up underneath the row of squares you are counting. If you do not purchase a stitch finder, you can use a strip of poster paper in the same way. A standing clear plastic book holder is also an asset, as your angle of vision on a chart is much better when the chart is upright than when it is lying down.

Charts can be either solid colored, color-coded, or both. There are advantages to each type of chart. A colored chart will give you a much better idea of how the finished piece will look, but it is sometimes difficult to see the lines of the chart. A color-coded chart has a symbol to represent each color in the design. If the color code indicates that the symbol x stands for gold, make a gold stitch for each x on the chart. Some color-coded charts are drawn in color—a green x stands for dark green, a green o stands for light green, a purple x stands for dark purple, a purple o stands for light purple, and so on. In this case, be sure to read the code key to get all the information available. When a chart is both colored and coded, it is usually to indicate intricate shading of the design.

Some experienced needleworkers help themselves count on a color-coded chart by marking lightly with a pencil those squares they have worked. When the needlework is finished, the pencil markings can be erased so that the chart may be used again.

*Work from the center out.* Begin counting at the center of the chart and stitching at the center of the material. Usually it is easier to work up from the center and complete the upper part of the design, then finish the lower part. However, it may be easier to outline a central figure, beginning with, or close to, the center stitch, then work to fill in the upper portions of the design, followed by the lower portions.

Find the middle of the chart by counting the number of squares up the height and the number of squares across the width. The place where the exact center of these lines cross each other is the center of the chart. Mark this center point on the chart.

Find the center of your canvas or cloth by folding it in half lengthwise, then again crosswise (Figure 1). Mark the center of the canvas or cloth. The safest method is with a sewing thread that can be snipped out after the work is begun. If you use a pencil, use it lightly. Never use a felt-tipped marker because it will bleed through the needlework.

The center of the chart may fall on one square of the design, or it may be somewhere in the background stitches. The center of the *chart* is not the same as the center of the *design*. You will, however, begin stitching from the center of the design. See the following examples (Figures 2, 3, 4) for how to start working a design from the center.

Work stitches, after the first stitch, to the right, left, or up, counting squares on the chart that are the same color and working the same number of squares in the same places on the canvas or cloth.

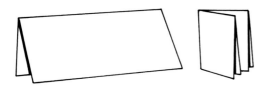

Figure 1. Find center of material by folding it in half lengthwise, then crosswise.

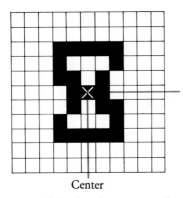

Center

Figure 2. If the center of the chart is one square, begin by making that stitch.

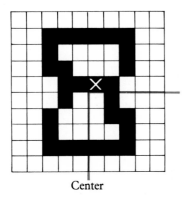

Center

Figure 3. If the center is a point where four stitches meet, choose either of the upper two squares and begin stitching.

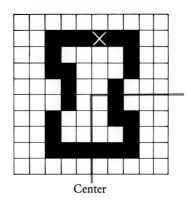

Center

Figure 4. If the center of the chart falls on the background, count up to the nearest design square and begin stitching there.

## Guides for Working Cross Stitch and Needlepoint

In cross stitch, each under stitch of the cross should slant from lower left to upper right, and the crossing upper stitch should slant from lower right to upper left. You may work all of the under stitches first, then go back and cross each (Figures 5a and 5b), or you may complete each cross stitch before beginning the next (Figure 6).

*For needlepoint* projects, use a tent stitch to work the design and a stitch of your choice to fill in the background. A tent stitch is any stitch which covers one thread intersection on top of the canvas and two thread intersections underneath: there are several versions of the tent stitch. Sometimes, it is necessary to change direction with your stitching; for example, you may need to change from working from left to right to working down. A half cross stitch will allow this to be accomplished. A half cross stitch in needlepoint covers one thread intersection on top of the canvas and only one thread intersection underneath. See the red stitches in Figure 7 for examples.

When possible, in an area of many stitches of the same color, use the diagonal tent stitch, also known as the basketweave (Figure 8). This stitch is one of the strongest of the tent stitches and distorts the canvas less than most other stitches as it is worked.

A suggestion for a background stitch is the diagonal mosaic stitch. It fits in particularly well with the slant of the tent stitch, and speeds up boring background work (Figure 9).

*Topstitching*, or backstitching, is indicated on a graph by lines. Finish the cross stitches or needlepoint stitches before working the topstitching. Use less yarn for topstitching on needlepoint by separating yarn strands, or use a full strand of embroidery floss. Top stitches may run along the sides, above, below, or diagonally across needlepoint and cross stitch stitches. They should be made by a "punch and stab" motion, not by "needle-through" (Figure 10).

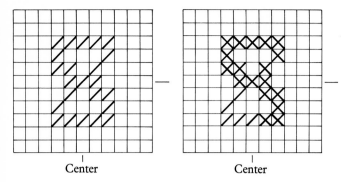

Center          Center

Figures 5a & 5b. Work all the stitches for the under stitch of the cross stitch from lower left to upper right; then make upper stitch from lower right to upper left.

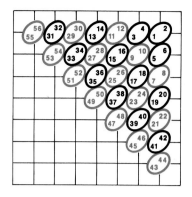

Figure 8. The diagonal tent stitch, also called the basketweave, should be used for backgrounds and any design areas that have many stitches of the same color. After the first three stitches, the rows drawn in black are worked diagonally down, with the needle put through the canvas vertically. Rows of stitches drawn in red are to be worked diagonally up, putting the needle through the canvas horizontally. Remember that the needle comes up from underneath the canvas on the odd numbers and goes in from the front on the even numbers.

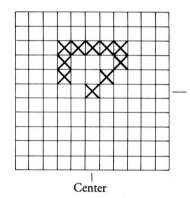

Center

Figure 6. Or, work each cross stitch completely as you go.

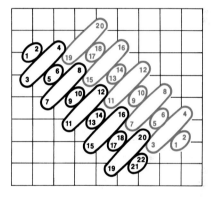

Figure 9. Follow the numbers for stitching the diagonal mosaic stitch.

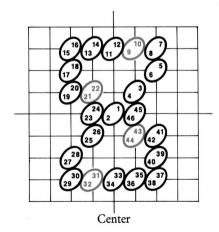

Center

Figure 7. To follow any stitch diagram, bring the needle up from underneath the canvas on odd numbers, (1, 3, 5) and put the needle through from above on even numbers (2, 4, 6). (Red stitches indicate half cross stitches.)

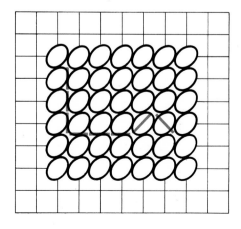

Figure 10. Embroidery stitches are worked after needlepoint is completed.

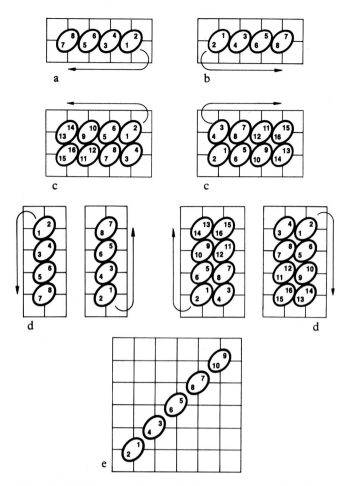

Figure 11. (a) This tent stitch is called the continental stitch. (b) If you must work from left to right, use a "stick and stab" rather than "needle through" method. Make sure each row of stitches slants in the same direction. (c) Two rows can be worked at once. (d) Illustrated also is how to work the tent stitch vertically, in single and double rows. (e) To work a single row of tent stitches slanting from lower left to upper right, use a "stitch and stab" motion, not "needle through".

## Choosing Colors and Materials

*When choosing colors,* don't hesitate to change from those of the printed charts. The charts are colored so that the contrasts are easier to follow when counting. Often, the shading could be made more gradual for a more sophisticated finished piece. It is in the choosing of colors, materials, and use that the needleworker creates an original piece of work from a printed chart. But keep in mind the one rule that will result in an interesting and alive product. There must be at least one very dark and at least one very light *tone* in the colors used. Other color tones may range from dark to medium to light. But without the contrast of a very light and a very dark, the design will be uninteresting.

There are no colors that are "wrong" used together, just as there are no color combinations that are "better" than other color combinations. Any combination of any colors, muted and subdued or bright and contrasting, is "right" if you like it.

*When selecting the materials* that you use for needlework, rely on your past experience and the advice of other needleworkers. Penelope canvas with a woven vertical thread and double horizontal threads is the most durable. Antique (beige) colored canvas is less likely to show canvas through the finished work than white canvas. If you use a mono canvas, which is easier to see than penelope, make sure that it is interlocking. This will insure even stitches. The mono canvas used for bargello stitches is not suitable for needlepoint.

You may use tapestry yarn, spun for needlepoint, or Persian yarn.

There are many materials used for count-thread cross stitch. The only absolute requirement is that the cloth be evenly woven ... that is, that there be as many threads in an inch horizontally as there are threads in an inch vertically. The number of threads from a strand of the embroidery floss that you use depends upon the weight of the cloth used.

# Your Favorite Craft Made Easy
# with Oxmoor House Family Guidebooks

### NEEDLECRAFT KINGDOM
*Adalee Winter*

The more than 100 original patterns presented in this book are worked out in graph form which can be adapted to different stitchery techniques — needlepoint, embroidery, knitting, quilting, mosaics and beadwork. Many of the patterns are illustrated in color. Subjects include children, butterflies, animals, birds, scenes from around the world and geometrics. Several completed needlecraft projects are pictured in color photographs. 64 pages. (413) $3.95.

### COUNTRY QUILT PATTERNS
*Mary Elizabeth Johnson*

This colorful book offers 23 never-before-published quilt block designs based on the common theme of our rural heritage. Each original design is featured in full color with complete instructions for construction including quilting and piecing diagram and pattern. Also included is a story by each designer describing how her design came into being. Highlighting the book are color photographs of several of the original designs made up into finished quilts. 80 pages. (478) $3.95.

### CREATIVE CRAFTS
Editors of *Southern Living* Magazine

A how-to book offering patterns and complete instructions in line drawings and step-by-step photographs for 24 small projects. Among the projects are wooden toys, a bonsai container, leather belts, a macrame plant container, a small loom, printed wrapping papers and a wine rack. 95 pages. (277) $1.95.

### NEEDLECRAFT PATTERNS
*Adalee Winter*

Winner of the National Needlepoint Guild's Book of the Year award, this book features 112 original patterns for needlepoint, embroidery, knitting, quilting and piecing, mosaics and beadwork. Each design is worked out in a graph pattern for easy application to the different stitchery techniques. The patterns include the alphabet, animals, flowers, birds and holiday motifs, many illustrated in color. Color photographs picture numerous completed projects using the patterns in the book. 60 pages. (241) $3.95.

### RELIGIOUS DESIGNS FOR NEEDLEWORK
*Adalee Winter*

Featured in this book are 77 splendid religious designs for home, church or synagogue. All of the designs are originals, and 32 are presented in full color. Each design is charted for easy application using different stitching techniques — needlepoint, cross stitch, embroidery or mosaic. Included are suggestions for various projects using the designs, and numerous completed projects are pictured in color photographs. 64 pages. (470) $3.95.

If your bookstore, homecenter, or supermarket does not carry these other Oxmoor House ''How-to'' books, you may mail order directly from the publisher by filling in the form below.

- - - - - - - - - - - - - - - - - - - - - - - - - - - - - - - - - - - - - - - - - - - - - - - -

# FAMILY GUIDEBOOK ORDER FORM

Please list quantity, title, code number, and price. If you include payment with the order, publisher will pay postage and handling. Otherwise add 75¢ for each book ordered. Any book in good condition may be returned within 30 days for full refund of purchase price. Send check or money order and allow 30 days for shipment.

| Qty. | Title | Code | Price | Post. | Total |
|------|-------|------|-------|-------|-------|
|      |       |      |       |       |       |
|      |       |      |       |       |       |
|      |       |      |       |       |       |
|      |       |      |       |       |       |
|      |       |      |       |       |       |
| Total |      |      |       |       | * |

(Prices subject to change without notice.)          *Alabama residents pay 4% sales tax.

My check or money order for _____ is enclosed.
Publisher pays postage and handling.

Charge $ _____ to my bank account. BankAmericard / master charge (Circle card.)

Charge signature _____

Name _____
(Please print clearly)

Address _____

City _____ State _____ Zip _____

Acct. No. _____ Exp. Date _____

Master Charge 4-Digit Bank No. _____
(lower left of card)

# OXMOOR HOUSE FAMILY GUIDEBOOKS

|  | Code | Price |
|---|---|---|
| **BUILDING & REMODELING** | | |
| Decks and Patios | (452) | $2.95 |
| Easy Home Carpentry | (373) | $1.95 |
| Easy Home Plumbing | (404) | $1.95 |
| Easy Home Remodeling | (405) | $1.95 |
| Easy Kitchen Remodeling | (387) | $1.95 |
| Floors and Floorcoverings | (451) | $2.95 |
| Home Paint Book | (403) | $1.95 |
| Home Security | (388) | $1.95 |
| Home Storage | (386) | $1.95 |
| Paneling & Wallcoverings | (442) | $1.95 |
| Saving Home Energy | (382) | $2.95 |
| **REPAIRS** | | |
| Easy Auto Repairs | (380) | $1.95 |
| Easy Electrical Repairs | (364) | $1.95 |
| Emergency Home Repairs | (372) | $1.95 |
| Furniture Repair & Refinishing | (378) | $1.95 |
| Outboard Boat and Motor Maintenance and Repair | (363) | $1.95 |
| **COOKBOOKS** | | |
| Best of Party Cookbook | (396) | $1.95 |
| Boating Cookbook | (283) | $1.95 |
| Breads Cookbook | (406) | $1.95 |
| Cakes Cookbook | (408) | $1.95 |
| Casseroles Cookbook | (357) | $1.95 |
| Chicken Cookbook | (409) | $1.95 |
| Cookies Cookbook | (360) | $1.95 |
| Country Cooking | (284) | $1.95 |
| Fish and Shellfish Cookbook | (359) | $1.95 |
| Inflation Cookbook | (275) | $1.95 |
| Party Snacks Cookbook | (358) | $1.95 |

|  | Code | Price |
|---|---|---|
| Preserving Foods | (375) | $1.95 |
| Salads Cookbook | (367) | $1.95 |
| Soups and Stews | (381) | $1.95 |
| Vegetable Cookbook | (365) | $1.95 |
| **GARDENING & LANDSCAPING** | | |
| Azaleas | (287) | $2.95 |
| Flowering Trees, Shrubs & Vines | (412) | $2.95 |
| Growing Flowers | (371) | $2.95 |
| Growing Lawns & Ground Covers | (383) | $2.95 |
| Growing Plants in Containers | (440) | $2.95 |
| House Plants | (384) | $2.95 |
| Landscaping Your Home | (285) | $2.95 |
| Vegetable Gardening | (410) | $2.95 |
| **HOBBIES & CRAFTS** | | |
| A Catalogue of the South | (366) | $4.95 |
| Country Quilt Patterns | (478) | $3.95 |
| Creative Crafts | (277) | $1.95 |
| Needlecraft Kingdom | (413) | $3.95 |
| Needlecraft Patterns | (241) | $3.95 |
| Religious Designs for Needlework | (470) | $3.95 |
| **TRAVEL & RECREATION** | | |
| Charley Dickey's Deer Hunting | (475) | $3.95 |
| Charley Dickey's Dove Hunting | (385) | $2.95 |
| Charley Dickey's Bobwhite Quail Hunting | (362) | $3.95 |
| Charley Dickey and Fred Moses' Trout Fishing | (376) | $2.95 |
| Jerry McKinnis's Bass Fishing | (361) | $2.95 |

Oxmoor House®

**P.O. Box 2463**
**Birmingham, Alabama 35202**